THERAPY HAD A
WAITING LIST
...SO HERE I AM

Therapy Had A Waiting List ...So Here I Am

Jeremiah King

Contents

Dedication

I want to dedicate this book to anyone who is just trying to evolve to their highest self. This book is simply just dedicated to those who want to be a better person. I hope something I've shared helps you in some way, it would make writing it worth it. If not for nothing, hope it just helps you feel less alone.

Introduction

Let me keep it all the way real by telling you I hated every moment of writing this outside of the Lessons Learned section. I love to write but writing down all my issues and trying to find out the root of that problem was not fun and it was very draining. I started this book in 2019 and I had over 200 pages written but it was headed in a different direction. 2020 happened and by the time 2021 came around I was really feeling like I needed to seek out some help.

Through my insurance I reached out to the therapists that were available and everyone had a waiting list but said online therapy was available. I only wanted to do therapy if I could sit down and build a connection with someone, something a little more intimate than online. That's when I scrapped my version of the book and decided to write down the things I didn't like about myself and then find out why. The title was then born "Therapy had a waiting list so here I am".

I've dragged my feet and procrastinated for two more years for many reasons I listed inside this book. I thought it was stupid and no one wants to read that; I didn't want to do the work mentally that it took to write it, I just wanted to be creative and this didn't feel creative, it felt like work. But I felt in my gut I could not move forward in my life and pursue some of my other passions until I completed this task, so here I am.

I pray God grants me a long life, so I can look back and see all these problems as problems far in the past. I hope my sons read this one day and have no idea who this man is. That will prove that I did the work to become who I desired to be. Anyways, turn the page and see what I'm rambling on about....

P.s. Thank you for taking time out of your life to read this, it means the world to me.

Anger

VIOLENCE comes naturally.

Peace
does
not.

My anger issues are embarrassing
at times,
but of course being
Embarrassed only makes me
more angry.

A disgusting cycle, I'm failing...

I'm upset you got in the way of becoming who you wanted to be.

The desire to evolve weighs so heavy on me.

I'm constantly putting myself down because I make the same
mistakes over and over--

Got a few things I really HATE about myself.

Why can I give out so much
                            positive energy to other people
                                            but never for myself?

The desire burns EVOLVE EVOLVE EVOLVE!

But the actions rarely follow the thoughts,

                                            pissed-

It's all my fault.

I've watched someone get stabbed,
        someones head get busted open,
        holes punched in walls,
        shootouts, screaming, cussing,
        fights, fights, fights.

The more violence I seen
the less I feared it and the angrier I got.

I don't sleep too well anymore.

For years my brain won't
shut up

I live a life of using nothing
as a crutch to help me live.

Ask me how well that's
working out for me

Why can't I be normal?

I forget how my inner voice sounds
                  because
                          I let too many voices distract me.

Why did you try to leave me?

That arm laying in the hallway from the bathroom at the top of the steps,   my mind can't erase.

Nothing but the light from the bathroom was on, as you mumbled my name for help.

Empty pill containers as you point to the address book for a phone number.

Hello confusion.

This was the first time you tried to leave me;

My child mind could not understand that it may have had nothing to do with me,
I blamed myself.

Gun in your hand, door locked.

Screaming on the phone, I pick up after you hung up.
Instructions to run to the neighbors for help!

My legs felt they couldn't run fast enough; in fear I would
hear
the gunshot before I could get help.

Cops arrive and take you in for evaluation
and I go to your friends house

I pretended to be asleep when you came in to hug me.

The   A n g e r   Grew.

I see a lot of people commenting on what it means to be biracial.

Who are in fact not biracial.

Will I cry at your funeral, when I barely know who you are?

Will our relationship ever heal so we can build from the
scar?

Hard to accept you left me for drugs or whatever else--

Addiction is a disease, but I've lost sympathy to help;

Forgive me for my honesty and also lying all these years.

Pray God teaches me how to raise my sons and remove all my fears;

Looking at old photos shows me this wasn't your plan.

Maybe you didn't receive the love you needed to grow from a boy to a man;

I was your biggest fan and then I grew up.

Santa's not real &
    your daddy isn't showing up.

You can't expose me to all this trauma as a kid and then I grow up and you say,

"I don't know what his problem is."

If I express how I am feeling then told to get out of my feelings,

Then let's see you do the same when I'm found hanging from the ceiling.

Trying to call the police, ripped the phone out of the wall;
Tried to leave in the car, you held onto the car.

FEAR

Dog tore up all the Christmas ornaments, your anger took over, but you called it discipline…

Who taught you that?

Drunken nights, slaps heard, screams loud, defenseless.
Huge fights, holes in the wall, you cried on the kitchen floor.
First time I seen a man cry; anger and regret went hand in hand with you.
I was so scared of you, but I sat on that kitchen floor because I didn't want to see you sad…

just wanted to help.

It was in these times that I observed how to deal with anger….violence.

My hatred is growing, I'm losing my soul.

Thirteen.
Getting high is starting to take its toll
On my mind;
and my words, I'm so disrespectful.
I'm going to end up just like him if I'm not careful.

Seeing my mother's face in that visitation room broke me because she was repeating the cycle, like father like son.

Even though I was in there for something I didn't do, I was spiraling.

Family started whispering,
                    I became the bad guy,
                                        fuck it, I'll play the role.

I needed support, I needed love,
                    instead, I got discipline not communication,

no one asked so I didn't explain,
                    further and further

                                                            I fell.

I shot, I was shot at
I fought, I won, I lost
I robbed, I stole, I cheated
Broke into houses holding onto morals
I followed until I learned how to lead
I was broken, I was lost, I was pissed off.

If you hurt my feelings I'll express it with anger;
If you embarrass me I'll express it with anger.

I'm aware of the problem.

And I'm aware I need to communicate the proper emotion,
Yet I never do.

Anger seems to be my comfort;
Until my least favorite emotion kicks in,

                                              ...regret.

The tv could never go loud enough to block out the screams of the neighbors;

The police lights brought the silence,
                                        But it never killed the noise.

Fear

Emotions get in the way but they're always here to stay.

The moment they are no longer here,

who would I become?

Terrified to find out who I am, if I no longer care.

That's a fear I don't choose to face;
So I'll be right here stumbling through my emotions.

I notice your fathers flaws
and I do my best to not repeat them.
So you aren't let down by two of the men who are supposed
to mean so much in a girl's life.

We spoke years ago, you apologized, and I said I forgive you.
But have I really...

when I hate the thought of being just like you.

He walked out my life-
You tried to end yours due to the pain that you were in-
I now understand that pain but at the same time I don't.

(I could never leave my sons in this world alone.)

I've been scared to write this
                              because you've came such a long way.
Just help me understand so I can move past these days.

                    You've taught me to be a caring man,
                Gave me memories that I can cherish for life.
Never pretended to be perfect and left your mistakes in
                                                        sight.

I love you for that.

You never physically left me but emotionally you checked out;
Closed off and cold; leaves my spirits down.

No secret I didn't like you when I was young, you didn't like
me as a teen;
But you chose to be in my life so you accept what that brings.

I've looked up to you in many ways you've taught me so much,
I hope I can teach you one thing if you don't see it as a crutch.

Like how to stop focusing on providing and focus on time;
Money comes and bills go but the clock is ticking on our life.

You have been such a light in my life,
I didn't know people like you existed.

Have you ever felt too dirty to talk to someone?
I don't want to ruin your life because I have a lot of baggage.

You are so pure,

So innocent.

So much love, you're ready to give and needing to receive;
I think this can work.

But I'm definitely scared.

My best friends
were murdered without us being on good terms.

You don't know what guilt really feels like,
I walk around drowning in regret.

So much
I feel I can
suffocate

at any
moment.

I hope I make my sons proud.

At the end of the day, I just want to be loved for who I am and not for what I do for you.

I most likely would not be alive if it wasn't for my kids.

Their love and its purity give me hope in life;
So much so that I now
Fear
Death.

I miss the innocence of being a child
Before corruption of this world crept into every inch of my
mind, body, but not soul...*I hope*

I'm terrified of my son's losing their innocence;
If there is one thing I wish to protect for all kids in the world,
it would be protecting them from the people looking to rob them of their innocence.

I cannot kill myself,
Because I am not rich enough.

What would I look like leaving my family
traumatized and broke.

I'm not going to do it;
but it worries me that the thoughts still enter my mind
when I'm depressed.

I don't want to talk, I just wanna do what I want to do with zero interruptions. I want to stay off my phone. Tired of feeling so bored that all I do is scroll. I'm not working towards anything, just simply getting through my days. I haven't been depressed in a while but have been sick of not having direction in my life. I have zero clue what to focus on. These bible plans aren't helping and God isn't speaking which makes me not want to read anything. I don't like this feeling, I have a lot of anger but I'm trying so damn hard not to yell anymore. I have no clue what the hell my life is supposed to be at this point, I guess I'm just here.

4/20/22

Though you shocked me.

This feeling is familiar.

Whole heartily trusting someone for years was strange for
me.

Unfortunately, one eye open is normal for me.

Everyone will let you down
just give them
time.

The person I desire to be is on the other side of discipline
but yet,

I never stay consistent long enough to meet him.

I hope I don't ruin my kid's childhood....

I don't think I could live with myself;

if I played a part in that.

I hope my sons don't get my dark mind, I hope they NEVER
experience
depression.
I hope they are more like their mother.

What if all that we believe in turns out to be a lie when we die?

That's still not something I'm willing to roll the dice on.

Lust

I'm in love with Lust.

I'm aware of the consequences that could come but in Lust
mode I'm immune until I cum.

Then I want to be far
away from
it.

I'm pure again.

I'm a great man.

And a short time passes and I'm chasing it again;
I don't do drugs,
don't have an alcohol problem,

But Lust robs me of who I desire to be.

I cheated on every
woman I've said
I Loved.

An addiction to feeling needed
caused me to seek
affection and attention
when I honestly had it in the partners,
I said I loved.

What does that say about my love?

If it gives me guilt then I don't want it.

I desire for every action I commit, every word I speak to be with a pure heart and a sane mind.

    Temporary pleasure is not worth a lifetime of guilt.

    Unfortunately, I ignore that when I'm horny.

Sexual urges,

lustful thoughts,

I can scroll through photos and find everything I'm looking for.

But the moment I give in, that's another woman I let down.

I'm added to the list of "those men"

Why am I willingly trying to live up to strangers' expectations?

Why are my partner's expectations not enough for me?

Why do I need every woman to not put me in the category as every other man?

Why can't it just be about my pleasure for a change?

Why do I care?

What would I tell my kids?

...Morals

Little did I know that a relationship I had in my teens,
for 3 years,
would shape my entire adult dating life.

How I viewed women, trusted women, what I hated about
myself, what I hated in my partner.

The good, the bad, the ugly;
I learned in that relationship.

How much sex is too much sex?

When does it become an addiction?

Because I felt I wasn't doing anything different than everyone I knew.

But the number of women I have been with is not ok, or is it?

I've wasted so much valuable time watching porn.

It's honestly ridiculous

How many more times do I have to fail
until it finally clicks?

How many more regrets do I have
to create until I stop thinking with
my dick?

When I was 4 my biological dad handed me a magazine like 'here look at these naked women because I won't have my son to grow up and be gay.'

Then I go to school wanting to touch on these girls.
Then I grow up nothing different than a squirrel-
Trying to chase a nut off a nice butt say whatever I need to say so she would let me fuck.

I thought I was the man with all these women,
I've given so much of myself away I feel broken.

The first person to teach me how to touch myself was my mom's boyfriend's son, when I was 6. He tried to touch me but as confused as I was I knew it didn't feel right because I wasn't attracted to boys.
I would later get whooping's when I got caught with my girl cousin;
Or another whooping when I walked up to the nearby building so my neighbor's daughter could show me how girls pee.
I was having girls flash me in 4th grade.
I was fingering girls by 6th grade.
I was going down on girls by 9th grade.
I was having sex by 15.

And none of these experiences were conversations I had with my parents.

As uncomfortable as it is to have that conversation, you have to talk with your kids.

I honestly don't know if it would have
changed my path but
I'll never know.

Insecurities

Constantly chasing perfection before I release
anything into the world.
A part of me feels I need to be sinless
before I'm worthy to speak.

I feel I am wasting potential
that I don't know
if it's there
anymore.
When I think high of myself, I feel as if I shouldn't.
But when I speak low I feel
as I should be more positive.

I don't have a goal weight.

I have a goal of being consistent.

Consistently   being   healthy.

I need to know you feel it too.

Before I step off this ledge, I need to know you'll be my
parachute,
Sometimes we all need an escape from this war.

The war in the mind,
How can we escape time?

By death I've been told.

But we alive right now,
so we got time to figure it out.

Are you with me or not?

I'm a grown man still wanting my
Father
to be proud of me

But even if he says he is
I
wouldn't believe it

What's my issue?

Some days I wake up and feel I can accomplish anything.

And other days I feel like the high school dropout that I am.

Who will ultimately fail his family.

I don't know at what point
food became my comfort,
but it always fails its job.

My feelings have been crushed multiple times but never felt the pain from a heartbreak in a relationship.

Until that morning...
Is it karma, probably.
Am I a hypocrite, maybe,
But I never saw this coming.

Not you.

I trusted you 100 percent which never happened in my life.

Now I know,
Trust Kills Kings.

I'm a romantic.

          But yet I don't know if I can fully articulate what
                  love is in a romantic relationship.

I just know I can't and don't want to do life without you.

More than needing you
                I want you.

                    I *believe* in this.

I don't understand the constant chase of perfection or where that started for me.

But let me break the fourth wall by saying,

I don't know what the hell this book is supposed to be.

I started in 2019 and have rewrote it four times.

One minute I'm going to tell my whole life story like a testimony;

And the next moment it's going to be like song lyrics, and then poems, and then quotes and then back to bio.

And then, and then, and then...

And then I say just be honest and vulnerable and it will reach who it needs to reach.

I've learned how hard it is to get back on the train
once you've been off

Mainly because maybe you got off before you ever
reached your destination.

Do I actually want to be with you,
Or does my ego just not want someone else to sleep with you?

I asked you what you Love about me,
    and I really never have gotten a clear answer.

Questions

Is there a raven and dove in us all?
Is our flesh the raven
Our spirit the dove
And our soul picks a side in the end?
Is it that simple or more complex?

How do you stay present when you want to get to the future, you?

See I want to be present for my kids, my wife, I love to be present and slow time down for everyone but myself.

It's like I want the future me in the present with my family although the only way to get to the future me is to take the steps now in the present moment...make sense?

Why do we
remember
the
traumatic
times in our
life more
than the
joyous
times?
Is trauma
the most
important
thing in
our life
journey?

What is it about myself that makes
people want to vent to me?

A lot of times they don't want advice,
they just want me to listen.

As honored as I am that so many
people trust me.

It can be draining when I have no one
I can pour out to.

Who do I vent to when no one will
listen to me without interjecting their
problems?

Am I wrong to want more for you then I think you want for yourself?

I'm no therapist,

       but I'd guess,

              a therapist would tell me that my pursuit

of seeing how many women I can get to desire me
Stems from abandonment issues and never feeling wanted by
my family.

What I could never figure out is why one woman desiring
me could never feel that void, what do you think?

How do you know when you are healed?
Is therapy never ending?

Questions in this book are not rhetorical.

Therefore, if you have an opinion let me know.

Communication is a beautiful thing.

I'm trying to grow.

I need water to do that...

What is it about
water and nature
that allow me to think?

I feel refreshed
and clear when I am
inside them.

Will being rich ruin me?

How many people are actually honest with themselves?

How can my heart be so full of love when I am with my kids
but so down and dark when I am alone?

Lessons Learned

Don't fiction me just give me the facts,

Because when I start wondering I don't know how to act.

So, don't fiction me just give the facts,

I don't need creamer, I drink my coffee black.

So many years,
A lot of lessons I've learned,
A lot of losses I've taken,
A lot of bridges have been burned.

I've learned forgiveness through betrayal,
Joy from pain.
Gratitude through Loss,
Pride through shame.

Much love has been created but with that comes hate.
You can't have one without the other that's the
ying and the yang.

No longer striving for perfection only focused on peace.

A calm spirit is a wise spirit;
Anger equals defeat.

I am no saint, but I am a son.

Watch how bettering yourself

affects and offends

so many others.

Dysfunction looks like fun for those who don't come from dysfunction,

But also;
Dysfunction can feel like home for so many who grew up in it.

My soul can't afford the price of your stubbornness.

Learn to meditate in the middle of the chaos.

Oftentimes, meditation is shown in peaceful environments but when do you need to meditate the most?

In the middle of the storm.

Why do we pass down the baggage of our parents' teachings and wrap it in Gold as gospel...

We ask when does the cycle end, instead of freeing ourselves to some of the chains wrapped around our minds.

I left the pain, frustration, and stress at the door, just as I did my shoes so they wouldn't track in mud.

I can not track my negativity across the floor and expect my child not to get messy.

If I was in the ocean drowning and I saw a boat of people nearby I would not hesitate to scream for help.

Yet every day we drown in our minds but let our pride prevent
us from screaming out for help.

Not everyone can afford therapy and drugs are a temporary escape.

Communication and honesty could save your life;
If only you will open your mouth and speak.

Never compromise the quality of your voice
for the quantity of just saying anything to not be forgotten.

Don't let fear force you to lose your integrity,
For your integrity is more valuable than any amount of
money.

Vulnerability is real strength.

The moment you step into the unknown emotion is the moment you become brave.

Trust can kill kings, but isolation can too.

Forgiveness is the bridge standing between me and you.

It's not about how much money you make, it's about how you spend it.

Just like it's not about how much life you have left, it's about how you use it.

Unlike money, time cannot be made again.

Time is your biggest luxury spend it accordingly.

I haven't reached my destination because I keep pulling off to rest at pit stops.

But all that does is *prolong my arrival.*

Sometimes you have to admit that you are your biggest problem.

You can have the life you want if you focus on your lane
or keep crashing trying to merge into others,

Keep your eyes on the road ahead and
the path will be
made clear.

You look at what
you can get,

I look at what
I can give.

You're scared to
lose followers,

I'm scared of
losing myself.

The most powerful things in this world are unseen.

I overthink but I don't overshare,

Learn how to be *silent.*

My mother never bashed my father,

and she had every right to;

That shows her character.

She tried to protect me at all costs even if it meant,

me turning on her;

What strength that shows, what love, what heart!

There are mountains and valleys in every relationship...

Just promise me you'll keep hiking.

I'll remember all you've
taught me,
I'll remember all you've
done.
I'll remember the way you
loved me,
And I'll honor the beautiful
human you were.

All this worrying is good for
nothing,
All this worrying is just
wasting time.
Promise me you'll go enjoy
heaven.
You lived your life now
I gotta live mine.

I'm the same person I've always been; is not a flex.

You should constantly evolve.

Before the kids, it was just you and me and once they grow that's still what it will be.

I loved you then, now, and forevermore.

Through every phase and change,

You are my muse.

I'm fully aware I have more to learn,

I will mature,

I will grow.

Today's understanding might not be tomorrow's understanding.

Children are leaders of today.

Follow the kid's they know the way.

Stop going against the current and learn to flow with it;

It will take you where you need to be.

But sometimes where you need to be is not where you
want to be but trust.

Life is always about perspective.

All of all,
can't be all of all,
of everything.

Find the thing that brought you *pure joy*
when you were a child and do it again
now.
The key to a lot of our happiness is finding
our inner child
and reconnecting to that person.

Conclusion

I've done ⅔ of the work so far. I identified the problem, got to the root of the problem but the goal is to change the problem or should I say transform.

I have so many things I want to accomplish in this life for myself, my sons, my wife, ect. In order to get those things accomplished I feel this was the first step. So maybe this helps you start doing the work yourself, I want us all to flourish and reach our highest potential.

I'm a very proud father and husband so much so; I lost who I am or who I desire to be. I can say writing this has helped clear the smoke and I'm starting to see the road ahead. I am happy, love you all!

-Jeremiah King

Author

Jeremiah King, born and raised
in Indianapolis, Indiana.
A husband and father
of two amazing boys.

Printed in the USA
CPSIA information can be obtained
at www.ICGtesting.com
LVHW021132201023
761655LV00077B/3170

9 798218 286996